D

Edith Kermit Carow Roosevelt

Edith Kermit Carow Roosevelt

1861–1948

BY Barbara Silberdick Feinberg

CHILDREN'S PRESS®
A Division of Grolier Publishing
New York   London   Hong Kong   Sydney
Danbury, Connecticut

Consultants: JOHN A. GABLE, PH.D.
The Theodore Roosevelt Association
Oyster Bay, New York
LINDA CORNWELL
Learning Resource Consultant
Indiana Department of Education

Project Editor: DOWNING PUBLISHING SERVICES
Page Layout: CAROLE DESNOES
Photo Researcher: JAN IZZO

Visit Children's Press on the Internet at:
http://publishing.grolier.com

Library of Congress Cataloging-in-Publication Data
Feinberg, Barbara Silberdick
     Edith Kermit Carow Roosevelt / by Barbara Silberdick Feinberg
        p.   cm. — (Encyclopedia of first ladies)
     Includes bibliographical references and index.
     Summary: Describes the childhood, family life, and marriage of the woman who
became the second Mrs. Theodore Roosevelt and eventually First Lady when he became the
twenty-sixth president of the United States.
     ISBN 0-516-21001-7
     1. Roosevelt, Edith Kermit Carow, 1861–1948—Juvenile literature. 2. Presidents'
spouses—United States—Biography—Juvenile literature. [1. Roosevelt, Edith Kermit Carow,
1861–1948   2. First ladies. 3. Women—Biography] I. Title II. Series.
E757.3.R65S25   1999
973.91'1'092—dc21   98–45243
[B]   CIP
                                                     AC

GROLIER
PUBLISHING

Table of Contents

Edith Kermit Carow Roosevelt

CHAPTER ONE

Childhood Sweethearts

☆ ☆ ☆ ☆ ☆ ☆ ☆ ☆ ☆ ☆ ☆ ☆ ☆ ☆ ☆ ☆

"I was but four years old when my mother came . . . to say that the Roosevelt children were coming to spend the day. I remember hiding my old and broken toys . . . ," Edith recalled as an adult. Did the four-year-old child want to impress her wealthy playmates? No one knows. She was a very private person and rarely spoke about her past. Much was written about the young Roosevelts, however. Because Edith Kermit Carow spent so much time with them, more is known about her childhood than she might have liked.

Edith's parents, the Carows, were an aristocratic New York family. Like the Roosevelts, they traced

☆ ☆ ☆ ☆ ☆ ☆ ☆ ☆ ☆ ☆ ☆ ☆ ☆ ☆ ☆ ☆

The Knicks

★ ★

Dutch fur traders were among the first to settle up and down the beautiful Hudson River Valley in present-day New York State. They founded New Amsterdam on Manhattan Island as a trading post and established farms and towns all the way up the river to Albany. They called it New Netherland, and it remained Dutch until the English took over in 1664 and created the colony of New York. Still, the region attracted Dutch settlers who left a lasting imprint on the landscape and the culture. Town names such as "Yonkers," words such as "cookie," and wonderful legends about the haunted New York mountains stay with us today. The "Knickerbocker" families are another legacy of the early Dutch. These wealthy Dutch settlers and their descendants were named for Diedrich Knickerbocker, a comic character created by author Washington Irving in his 1809 history of Dutch New York. Theodore Roosevelt descended from old Dutch "Knickerbocker" families. Today, however, some other Knickerbockers may be more familiar: New York's pro-basketball team, called "the Knicks" for short.

their ancestors back to colonial times. Charles Carow, Edith's father, was descended from French Protestants, or Huguenots, who escaped to North America in 1685 to gain religious freedom. They founded the successful shipping firm of Kermit & Carow. Her mother, Gertrude Tyler, was a descendant of New England preacher

Edith Kermit Carow's mother, Gertrude Tyler Carow

Connecticut, U.S.A.

✦ ✦

Edith Carow was born in the southeastern corner of Connecticut, the third-smallest state in the Union. Its name comes from an Indian word meaning "beside the long tidal river," a reference to the Connectictut River, which cuts the state just about in half. Settled by the strictest Puritans, this land was originally the home of the Mohegan tribe. In the 1600s, their famous chief Uncas helped settlers defeat the neighboring Narragansetts. By the year of Edith's birth two centuries later, many farmers had long since left the state for more fertile lands in the West. The "Connecticut Yankees" who remained busied themselves with industry and invention. The tiny state became fa-

Edith Carow was born in her grandfather Tyler's house in Norwich, Connecticut.

mous for clocks, locks, and guns; cottons and woolens; and many other factory-produced goods. A few miles south of Edith's birthplace, coastal communities such as Mystic and New London bustled with the nautical commerce of whaling fleets and clipper-ship builders. During Edith's childhood, however, Connecticut yielded its most priceless product. Of the 55,000 Connecticut troops to serve in the Civil War between 1861 and 1865, 20,000 were killed or wounded.

Jonathan Edwards. The Roosevelts, like other families whose ancestors were New York's early Dutch settlers, were called "Knickerbockers."

Gertrude and Charles were wed on June 8, 1859. Edith was born on August 6, 1861, at her grandfather's home in Norwich, Connecticut. By the time of her birth, the Southern states had seceded from the Union.

Portrait of America, 1861: Two Americas

✫ ✫

Upheaval and uncertainty marked the year that Edith Carow was born. Slavery and other disagreements tore the country apart. By 1861, 11 Southern states seceded from the Union to form the Confederate States of America. That left 23 states, including far-flung California and Oregon, and 23 million people in the North. The 11-state Confederacy included nearly 9 million people, about 3.5 million of whom were black slaves. A civil war between the two Americas would begin and last four bloody years. The first shots were fired on Fort Sumter in Charleston, South Carolina, on April 12, 1861.

Two presidents ruled over the divided nation. Abraham Lincoln was inaugurated as the sixteenth president of the Union. Just weeks before, Jefferson Davis had been sworn in as president of the Confederate States. Neither man could have imagined what lay ahead. Thinking the conflict could be ended quickly, Lincoln asked for 75,000 volunteers to enlist for three months. By the actual end of the war four years later, an estimated 2 million Northern soldiers had served.

Americans got their first taste of the terrible war to come on July 21 at the First Battle of Bull Run fought at Manassas Junction just outside of Washington, D.C. So confident were Northern supporters that many civilians drove out from the city with picnic lunches to watch the fight. They witnessed a frightening defeat. After the bloodshed, fleeing soldiers and carriages filled with terrified sightseers clogged the muddy roads back to the capital. Clearly, victory in this war would be difficult and costly.

While the South slipped away, many Americans were pushing west. By 1861, the frontier—that imaginary boundary between civilization and wilderness—lay just about down the middle of the continent from the western edge of Lake Superior to the southern tip of Texas. Kansas joined the Union as the newest free state, and the territories of Dakota, Colorado, and Nevada were organized. For the first time, 3,500 miles (5,633 kilometers) of telegraph line, called "Lightning

Wire," connected the East and West Coasts, eliminating the need for mail delivery by Pony Express.

While North and South prepared for war, Yale University awarded its first Ph.D. degree. Eccentric Matthew Vassar donated money he had made brewing beer and a little land to establish Vassar Female College in Poughkeepsie, New York. Thaddeus Lowe journeyed a record 900 miles (1,448 km) in a balloon, and the first pretzel factory opened in Pennsylvania. Patents were issued for 2,919 new inventions.

Though divided, the American spirit seems not to have dimmed.

Isaac Carow, Edith's paternal grandfather

The Civil War had begun. The war affected Edith's life when she was almost two. Her beloved grandfather, Brigadier General Daniel Tyler, left to fight with the Union forces in Mississippi. In 1864, when Edith's grandmother Emily Tyler died, the Carows moved to New York City.

Edith grew up as a member of the privileged upper class in the neighborhood surrounding Union Square Park. She first met Corinne Roosevelt, called "Conie," when their nursemaids took them to the park for airings. The girls were the same age and frequently visited each other's homes. While Edith was quiet and serious, Conie was lively and outgoing.

This view shows New York City from Union Square Park as it looked about the time Edith moved there in 1864.

Edith soon met the other Roosevelt children: Anna, or "Bamie," the oldest, Theodore, or "Teedie," and Elliott, or "Ellie." Conie was the youngest. The Roosevelts treated Edith as a member of their family and gave her a nickname too, "Edie." She quickly befriended the sickly Teedie, who often had difficulty breathing. She frequently played house with him,

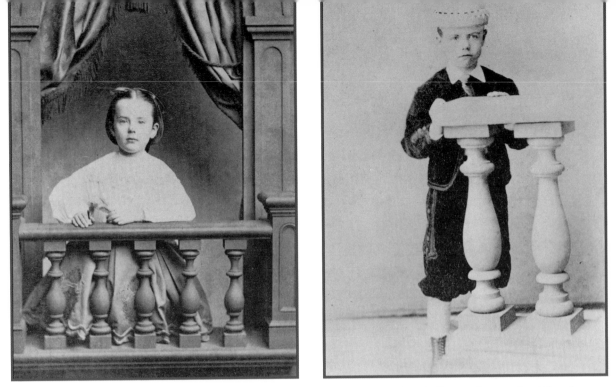

These photographs of Edith Carow (above left) and the Roosevelt children (Elliott, above right; Theodore, below left; and Corinne, below right) were taken about 1865, the year after Edith moved to the Union Square neighborhood of New York City.

Edith and the Roosevelt children watched Abraham Lincoln's funeral procession (above) as it passed the mansion owned by Theodore's grandfather.

Theodore Roosevelt's mother, Martha "Mittie" Bulloch (above), invited Edith to attend a kindergarten taught by Mittie's sister Anna Bulloch.

shooing away the more active Ellie. On April 18, 1865, Edith's sister Emily was born, but the two girls never developed a close relationship.

A week later, Edith—nearing her fourth birthday—and the two Roosevelt brothers were invited to Grandfather Cornelius Roosevelt's mansion to watch Abraham Lincoln's funeral procession on April 25, 1865. The children looked out a window and saw the marchers and horsemen escorting

the slain president to the train that would take him from New York to Illinois, his home state. Before he was assassinated, Lincoln had guided the Union to victory over the South. Edith, frightened by the noise and strange sights, began to cry. The boys made her leave the room.

By the time Edith was six, her father was no longer able to pay his bills. Charles, a scholarly man, was not suited for the family business and had

Mittie Roosevelt's sister Anna Bulloch taught kindergarten at the Roosevelt home.

become an alcoholic. To economize, the Carows moved in with relatives. Never again would they be able to afford to set up their own household. During the winter, they lived with Aunt Kermit in her home near Union Square. Grandfather Tyler invited them to his place in Red Bank, New Jersey, for the summer. Distressed by their circumstances, Edith's mother began to suffer a number of real and imaginary illnesses. She was relieved when Martha "Mittie" Roosevelt invited Edith to attend a kindergarten taught by Mittie's sister, Anna, at the Roosevelt home on East 20th Street.

Where Children Could Grow

✶ ✶

The concept of the "kindergarten," or children's garden, was born in Germany in the 1830s. This new approach to education was based on the revolutionary idea that children learned by playing rather than by memorizing and reciting. For a long time, children had been viewed and treated as little adults without special needs of their own. Now, kindergartens gave four- to six-year-olds a place where they could "unfold naturally, like flowers." Individual kindergartens (like the one Anna Bulloch ran in her home) began to appear in the United States in the 1850s. In 1873, St. Louis was the first to incorporate them into the school system. Today, nearly 4 million children attend kindergarten in the United States.

Teedie's father, Theodore, took Edith and the Roosevelt children on excursions to Central Park.

Anna taught Edith and the Roosevelt children to read from the McGuffey Readers, a collection of stories with moral lessons. Mittie, a Southerner, read to the children and told them tales of bygone plantation life. Edith acted in plays directed by Teedie's father, Theodore. Although he was busy with charity projects, Theodore took the children on nature trips along the Hudson River and boat rides in Central Park. Edith enjoyed these outings, but she did not share Teedie's passion for dissecting and preserving the insects, reptiles, and rodents they found. To strengthen the children, a gymnasium was built in the Roosevelt home. Edith made little effort to join her friends in their physical exercises because she was not good at parallel bars and ladders.

In 1869, Edith's mother enrolled her in Mr. Dodsworth's dancing classes. There she met other children from privileged families and learned to move in time to the music. She was also taught how to conduct herself in polite society. During the spring of 1870, when the Roosevelt children came home from a year spent in

Women of the Upper Crust

✯ ✯

Teedie and Edith grew up in the Gilded Age, a time of wealth and leisure for upper-class Americans. Theirs were families of "old money," made over generations of landownership and business success. With no income taxes to pay (there was no such tax until 1913), the rich could stay that way. These American "aristocrats" divided their time between summer and winter homes, enjoyed lavish parties, and spent money on elegant estates, fine clothes, and extensive travel. Their children attended the best schools and learned to dance and ride horses.

Women of this privileged class lived lives governed by expectation, tradition, and ritual. Supervising large staffs of servants, decorating their homes and themselves in the finest style, and entertaining occupied much of their time. Many made trips to Paris each year to purchase the latest French fashions. They were especially busy throughout the social "season," which ran from fall through the winter. Then, the most elegant parties were given, many of them to introduce marriageable young ladies into society. Much fuss was made, especially among eligible bachelors, over these "debutantes" as they "came out." Society mothers fussed, too, preparing their daughters to marry into "suitable" families and to bring honor to the family name as perfect hostesses, loving mothers, and skillful household managers. They believed that proper ladies were mentioned in the newspapers only three times in their lives: at birth, at marriage, and at death.

Europe, they, too, attended the classes. Edith and Teedie had written to each other while the Roosevelts were away.

The following year, Edith moved to a new home. New York's aristocratic and wealthy families were abandoning Union Square for more fashionable addresses uptown. The Roosevelts eventually settled on West 57th Street, but Aunt Kermit and the Carows could only afford to relocate in the less desirable West 40s. Nearby was the exclusive Miss Comstock's School, which Edith attended.

Edith and Teedie wrote to each other when Teedie was in Paris (above).

In the 1870s, wealthy families were moving from the Union Square neighborhood (right) for more fashionable addresses uptown.

Ten-year-old Edith thrived in school. Like the private tutors in the Roosevelt home, her teachers stressed proper conduct and good behavior. Edith excelled in Latin, with help from her father. To his delight, she shared his interest in studies of history and English literature. She developed a lifelong fondness for the works of William Shakespeare.

At school, Edith was more reserved than most girls her age, keeping her feelings to herself. She enjoyed her privacy and spent hours by herself reading and thinking. This prompted one classmate to write, "I believe you could live in the same house with Edith for fifty years and never really know her." After six years of study, Edith graduated from Miss Comstock's, her education completed. In the 1870s, girls from good families were expected to take their place in society, marry, and raise children, rather than go on to college or work.

In 1873, when Teedie and his family returned to New York from another year abroad, Edith took part in their activities once more. Conie formed a weekly literary club and re-

Edith (left) was appointed secretary of the literary club formed by Corinne (second from right).

cruited Edith as its secretary. The girls wrote stories and poetry, which they read among themselves. While Edith's stories dealt with true love and romance, her poems were filled with

Left to right: Teedie, Corinne, Edith, and Elliott about 1875 or 1876

Corinne (left) and Edith on the lawn of the Roosevelt's summer home in Oyster Bay about 1878

sadness and despair, perhaps reflecting her feelings about living with an alcoholic father, an invalid mother, and a difficult sister.

For the next three years, Edith divided her summers between her grandfather's house near Red Bank, New Jersey, and the Roosevelt's summer home on Oyster Bay, Long Island. In New Jersey, Edith swam and went for long walks. She collected wildflowers and could eventually identify most American species. At Oyster Bay, she participated in family activities: reciting poetry, acting in plays, swimming, and riding horseback. Teedie often took her around the bay in his rowboat, named *Edith*.

Teedie couldn't attend Conie's fifteenth birthday party, as he left that day to study at Harvard. Edith missed him and looked forward to Christmas when she could see him again. The following year, in May 1877, Teedie invited his sisters to Harvard for the weekend and asked them to bring Edith along. When they left, Teedie wrote to Conie, "I don't think I ever saw Edith looking prettier; everyone . . . admired her little Ladyship intensely, and she behaved as sweetly as she looked." Tall and fair haired, Edith always appeared to be spotless and perfectly groomed. The more-sociable Conie grew envious of Edith's intelligence and appearance as well as her friendship with Teedie.

The death of Theodore Roosevelt Sr. from cancer in February 1878 did not prevent his grieving family from spending the summer at Oyster Bay. Theodore, as Teedie now preferred to be called, was inseparable from Edith during her visit. On August 22, something happened to cause a break in their relationship, but we don't know what it was. Theodore seems to have proposed to Edith more than once

Teedie, now called Theodore, as a freshman at Harvard University

Theodore, active in sports at Harvard, is shown here in his rowing outfit.

Alice Hathaway Lee (left), Theodore, and Alice's cousin Rose Saltenstall about 1879

Edith and Theodore remained friends after Theodore married Alice Lee (above) in 1880.

during this time. She did not accept. However, whether a proposal was made that day or not, we don't know. In any event, they seemed to have quarreled. Edith never discussed what happened. Theodore later admitted that "we both of us had . . . tempers that were far from being the best." When Theodore returned to college,

he sought out other young women. He fell in love with the beautiful Alice Lee and secretly proposed to her in 1879. His friendship with Edith continued, but their romance ended. Remembering her temper, he wrote to Conie, "Give my love to Edith—if she's in a good humor; otherwise, my respectful regards."

Edith and her sister, Emily Tyler Carow (above) were never very close.

Edith was the first of Theodore's friends to be told about his wedding plans. She gave a dinner party for him and his bride-to-be. At the wedding in Boston, on October 27, 1880, the normally serious Edith danced "the soles off her shoes." She kept her regrets about the marriage to herself, but she was decidedly cool toward Alice when

they met at parties and teas. She treated Theodore, however, as a special longtime friend. They went for drives in the park, and she enjoyed talking with him. Before long, Edith also attended the weddings of Conie and Ellie.

Apart from her friends' marriages, Edith had little to celebrate. She faced a sad and uncertain future. Aunt Kermit had died in 1879, and the Carows had to stay with her surviving brother. Then Grandfather Tyler passed away in November 1882, leaving a modest sum of money to be paid to Edith's mother twice a year. Finally, in March 1883, Charles Carow died, weakened by alcoholism.

For all his faults, Edith loved her father and missed him very much. At his death, she had two choices. She could marry for money and security, or she could move with her mother and sister to Italy, where they could live more cheaply than in New York. Neither choice appealed to her. Edith never thought she would have a third choice, to marry the man she loved and become the second Mrs. Theodore Roosevelt.

CHAPTER TWO

The Second
Mrs. Theodore Roosevelt

★　★　★　★　★　★　★　★　★　★　★　★　★　★　★

"You know all about me darling. I never could have loved anyone else," Edith wrote to Theodore in June 1886, just months before her marriage to him. Years of separation had strengthened Edith's feelings for Theodore. After the tragic deaths of his mother and his wife on February 14, 1884, Theodore had retreated to his cattle ranch in the Badlands, now part of North Dakota. He left his sister Bamie in charge of his infant daughter Alice. Edith avoided seeing him when he returned to New York City for visits because she did not want to upset him. She knew that he felt uneasy about their adolescent romance and mourned his late wife.

★　★　★　★　★　★　★　★　★　★　★　★　★　★　★

Alice Hathaway Lee (1861–1884)

✦ ✦

The tall and slender Alice Lee captured young Theodore Roosevelt's heart when they met at the home of a mutual friend in October 1878. Alice was seventeen and came from a well-to-do Boston family. Harvard man Theodore's rough and ready ways contrasted with her quiet and cultured elegance. Friends recalled Theodore once exclaiming, "I am going to marry her. She won't have me, but I am going to have her!" And so they courted over the next months, and finally Alice accepted his proposal of marriage. They were wed on Theodore's 22nd birthday, October

27, 1880. Later, Theodore remembered their brief marriage as "three years of happiness such as rarely comes to man or woman." Theodore began his career in New York state politics. Soon, Alice became pregnant. Before the baby was born, Alice went to stay with Theodore's mother in her New York City apartment while Theodore tended to business in Albany. Then, double tragedy struck. Two days after his baby daughter, named Alice, arrived on February 12, 1884, Theodore's mother died of typhoid fever. His wife Alice died of kidney disease on the same day. A double funeral was held for the two Roosevelt women on February 16. "When my heart's dearest died, the light went from my life forever," wrote Theodore a year later.

In September 1885, they met accidentally at Bamie's home and were attracted to each other. After seeing Edith privately, Theodore started taking her to parties and dances where they were accepted as old friends, not lovers. They hid their feelings for each other in public, but on November 17, 1885, Theodore asked Edith to marry him. She accepted. Although Edith and Theodore had very different personalities, they were well-suited. She craved privacy, was self-disciplined, and put duty before pleasure. Theodore was outgoing, sociable, and at times impulsive. She steadied him, and he made her more lively. They were both intelligent and held high standards of personal conduct.

They told no one of their engagement. Society expected mourning to last several years, and Theodore feared he would appear unfaithful to his late wife. In the spring of 1886, he returned to ranching while Edith ac-

Above left: Theodore's daughter Alice in 1885

Left: Theodore's sister Bamie with his daughter Alice in 1886

Theodore returned to ranching in Dakota Territory in the spring of 1886, while Edith went to Europe with her mother and sister.

companied her mother and sister to Europe. During the summer, a newspaper gossip columnist revealed their engagement, but Bamie had the newspaper print a denial. An embarrassed Theodore admitted to her that the story was true. In the fall, Bamie and her brother sailed to England, where Theodore's marriage to Edith took place on December 2, 1886. The newlyweds immediately left on their honeymoon, touring France and Italy.

Returning to New York in March 1887, the Roosevelts made plans to settle permanently in Oyster Bay. They moved into the house Theodore had built for Alice. It had been called Leeholm after her family, but he renamed it Sagamore Hill to please his new bride. To please Theodore, Edith did not remove the masculine decorations including stuffed moose and elk heads, the results of his frequent hunting trips. She also insisted that his

During the Roosevelts' honeymoon in France and Italy, they may have eaten at the Café de la Régence on Paris's Rue St. Honoré (left).

Below: The Champs Élysées, Paris, as it looked when the Roosevelts were there

A view of Florence, Italy, from San Miniato, as it looked about the time of the Roosevelts' honeymoon trip

When the Roosevelts returned from their honeymoon, they moved into the house now called Sagamore Hill in Oyster Bay, New York.

daughter live with them. By mothering three-year-old Alice, Edith accepted Theodore's past. Theodore and Edith never talked about Alice's mother, however, and this proved confusing to the child.

In September 1887, Edith gave birth to a son, Theodore Roosevelt Jr. During the next ten years, she had four more children: Kermit in 1889, Ethel in 1891, Archibald in 1894, and Quentin in 1897. Unlike many privileged couples of their day, Edith and

Theodore were very involved in raising their children, reading them bedtime stories and encouraging their hobbies. The children were allowed to collect and keep a wide variety of pets, including Emily Spinach, a snake named for Edith's sister, and a bear called Jonathan Edwards, named for Edith's noted ancestor. The young Roosevelts, however, were not educated at home. They were sent to public school.

Although Edith expected her chil-

A July 1905 view of Edith Roosevelt's Sagamore Hill garden

Edith reading to Theodore Jr. and Kermit about 1891, not long before Ethel was born

dren to be polite to others, she was tolerant of their pranks. Girls usually played docilely with dolls while boys roughhoused. Edith, however, let Alice and Ethel join in their brothers' antics. One son even commented, "When Mother was a little girl, she must have been a boy!" In the years before radio, television, computers, and stereo systems, Edith nurtured her children's imagination and shared with them her interests in history, po-

A 1901 picture of Kermit, (left), Ethel, and Ted Roosevelt with their pet guinea pigs, among the Roosevelt children's many pets

Archibald (Archie) Roosevelt, Edith and Theodore's fourth child, on his pet pony, Algonquin

Edith's own nursemaid, Mame, is shown here with Quentin, the Roosevelts' youngest child.

Theodore (upper right) enjoyed playing outdoors with his children and their Roosevelt cousins.

etry, and wildflowers. Impressed by her knowledge, they asked her how she knew so much. She replied, "From that military gentleman, General Information." With help from her own nursemaid Mame, Edith also bandaged their scraped knees and comforted them when they had chicken pox and other childhood diseases.

To please Theodore, Edith learned to play tennis and to bicycle, but she did not enjoy these activities. Theodore usually romped with the children outdoors while she retreated to her sitting room to sew or read. He enjoyed playing with them so much that Edith called him "her oldest and rather worst child." He taught the children swimming and boating and took them for nature walks. Often, they were joined by some or all of their sixteen Roosevelt cousins. Among them was Theodore's niece Eleanor, the daughter of his brother Ellie who had died of alcoholism in 1894. Edith described her as "very plain. . . . But the ugly duckling may turn out to be a swan."

When she could leave the children, Edith enjoyed traveling. In September 1890, she visited Theodore's

Edith described Theodore's niece Eleanor as an "ugly duckling who may turn out to be a swan."

ranch in the Badlands. Like her husband, she loved the wild scenery and the isolation. From there, the Roosevelts toured Yellowstone National Park on horseback. In the East, it still was not acceptable for women to ride astride horses, but out West, the horses were unaccustomed to sidesaddles. Edith, an accomplished rider, was thrown from her sidesaddle when her horse was frightened by the sound of blasting. She escaped uninjured. On another trip, in 1893, the Roosevelts joined Bamie at the Chicago World's Columbian Exposition. The fair hon-

In September 1890, Edith visited Theodore's ranch in the Badlands and stayed in his cabin in Medora (right). From there, they toured Yellowstone National Park on horseback.

Edith and Theodore probably saw Yellowstone Park's Old Faithful geyser on their 1890 visit.

ored the 400th anniversary of Columbus's discovery of America. The colorful fireworks and the open-air concerts made Edith feel as if she were "in fairyland."

Growing up in the Carow household, Edith had learned to be frugal. Therefore, Theodore turned over to her responsibility for managing the family finances. He did not have a head for figures. The blizzard of 1887–1888 had destroyed his Western cattle herd and with it, much of the money his father had left him. To support his family, he turned to politics and wrote a number of books. Earlier, Theodore had served in the New York State Assembly, the lower house of the state legislature, or law-making body. He had also been the Republican party's unsuccessful candidate for mayor of New York City. As Theodore's political career progressed, Edith and the children grew accustomed to moving from city to city while spending summers in Oyster Bay at Sagamore Hill.

In 1889, the Roosevelts rented a house in Washington, D.C., while Theodore served as a civil-service commissioner. Under the reforms of 1883, he supervised the selection of public servants to carry out government programs. No longer would party leaders be able to reward their followers by giving them government jobs.

Chicago's Great White City

★ ★

A ticket to the Columbian Exposition

The Ferris wheel

All eyes turned to Chicago on May 1, 1893, for the opening of the dazzling World's Columbian Exposition. This was to be the greatest world's fair ever, held on 550 acres (223 hectares) along Chicago's lakefront. The grandeur of its gleaming white buildings gave it the name "White City." More than a million objects celebrated the world's progress in science, industry, and art since the voyage of Christopher Columbus four hundred years before. At precisely 12:08 A.M. on opening day, President Grover Cleveland pressed the master switch to electrify lights, fountains, and machinery. Never before had people witnessed such an awesome display of electricity, that mysterious new invisible power source. Besides electricity, all the wonders of the modern world thrilled the 21 million visitors who flocked to the fair that summer. Moving pictures, refrigeration, fine art, a ten-ton cheese, and the world's first wieners delighted fairgoers. For pleasure-minded visitors, sideshows lined the Midway. Exotic replicas of faraway places included the "Streets of Cairo" pavilion. There the famous belly dancer "Little Egypt" did the "hootchy-kootchy," distressing the proper ladies in the crowd. Most spectacular of all, the 250-foot (76-m) Ferris wheel towered above the grounds. An engineering marvel, the wheel symbolized both the fun and the wonder of the World's Columbian Exposition.

Left: The Art Palace at night

Bottom left: "The Watergate"

Below: The Administration Building

This picture of Edith was taken when Theodore was a civil-service commissioner.

Theodore Roosevelt as he looked when he served as a New York State assemblyman

The "spoils system" was forbidden. Now, jobs were filled by competitive exams.

It was expensive to run homes in two cities, but Edith did the best she could. The national economic downturn of 1893 made her task even more difficult. She searched for bargains in

Edith enjoyed hiking in Rock Creek Park (above) during her time in Washington, D.C.

plished hostess at her own dinner parties. She preferred the company of intellectuals and artists to socialites and politicians. Her closest friends were noted authors, historians, and sculptors of the day.

In 1894, Edith convinced Theodore to turn down an offer to run once more for mayor of New York City. She preferred the leisurely pace of the capital to the bustling activity in New York and was reluctant to leave her new friends. She did not know how much the election meant to Theodore. When she found out, she felt guilty that she had not encouraged him to enter the race. It was their first major misunderstanding in eight years of marriage.

In 1895, when Theodore accepted the post of president of New York City's Board of Police Commissioners, the family returned to Sagamore Hill. While he fought a losing battle to re-

local stores and allowed Theodore only $20 a day for spending money. Despite financial burdens, Edith enjoyed Washington. Hikes in Rock Creek Park and visits to the Smithsonian Institution's art collection pleased her. She attended many official receptions and became an accom-

Theodore Roosevelt was police commissioner of New York City from 1895 to 1897.

Theodore (second from left) with members of the board of police commissioners of New York City

form the corrupt police force, Edith was involved with the children. She remained calm upon hearing the news of her mother's death in Italy and did not encourage her sister to move in with her. Except for occasional visits to see Edith, Emily remained in Italy.

To Edith's delight, the family returned to Washington in 1897. Republican President William McKinley had appointed Theodore assistant secretary of the navy. While Theodore worked to make the United States a strong naval power, Edith took up the life she had left two years earlier. In December 1897, however, she became seriously ill with a high fever and an infection. When she did not recover, her doctors recommended an operation to remove a swelling in her ab-

President William McKinley appointed Theodore Roosevelt assistant secretary of the navy in 1897.

William McKinley (1843–1901)

★ ★ ★ ★ ★ ★ ★ ★ ★ ★ ★ ★ ★ ★ ★ ★ ★ ★ ★ ★

As the last Civil War soldier to be president and as the first president of the twentieth century, William McKinley represented the end of one era and the beginning of another. Born in Niles, Ohio, he served in the Union army under another president, Rutherford B. Hayes. He became a lawyer in 1867 and served many years as a Republican representative to Congress and then as governor of Ohio. In 1896,

he became the twenty-fifth president of the United States by campaigning from his front porch in Canton, Ohio. He was a gifted speaker, and more than 750,000 Americans came to hear him describe his plans for national prosperity. He is best remembered, however, for involving the nation in the Spanish-American War in 1898 and expanding America's role as a world power. McKinley was devoted to his wife Ida, with whom he shared the sadness of losing two daughters. Ida herself suffered from epilepsy, and her husband protected her during their years together in the White House. He even moved his office so that he could be closer to her sitting room. William McKinley was assassinated just months into his second term.

domen. Theodore preferred to wait, hoping to spare her a painful ordeal. The life-saving surgery was finally performed in March 1898, prompting him to write that "she behaved heroically."

Inflamed by reports of Spanish misrule in Cuba and by a mysterious explosion that destroyed the U.S. battleship *Maine* in Havana Harbor, the United States declared war against Spain in April 1898. Once Edith was out of danger, Theodore began to organize a volunteer cavalry unit to fight for Cuban independence. In May, he resigned from the government and headed for training camp in Texas. He knew his wife could manage the family without him. She hid her fears for his safety and supported his decision. She even visited him in Florida before he shipped out. Theodore became a national hero when he led his regiment of "Rough Riders" in a dramatic charge up Kettle Hill in Cuba under

Theodore carried this family picture with him during the Spanish-American War. From left to right: Theodore holding Archie, Ted and Alice standing, Edith holding Kermit and Ethel

The Spanish-American War: Fast Facts

WHAT: The Cuban war for independence from Spain

WHEN: Cuba had struggled for independence since the Ten Years' War of 1868 to 1878. Open revolt again broke out in 1895.

WHO: Cubans rebelled against their Spanish rulers. America entered the conflict in 1898 after the American battleship *Maine* blew up in Havana Harbor.

WHERE: U.S. troops fought the Spanish in naval and land battles in Cuba and the Philippines. At war's end, U.S. troops captured the Spanish colony of Puerto Rico.

WHY: The Cubans rebelled against Spanish rule. Americans clamored for military intervention, especially after the loss of the *Maine* with more than 260 American lives. Many Americans saw war with Spain as a way for America to become a world power.

OUTCOME: The war lasted 10 months. The U.S. victory had been relatively easy, but not without cost. While 385 men were killed in action, more than 5,100 died of disease and accident. The peace treaty granted Cuba its independence and the United States received Puerto Rico, Guam, and the Philippines from Spain.

The U.S. battleship Maine

enemy fire. When he returned, Edith hoped he would retire from politics and write books. However, the popular Theodore Roosevelt (now often referred to by the press and the public as Teddy or TR), accepted an offer from New York Republicans to run for governor and won.

In 1899, the Roosevelts moved to Albany, the state capital. At the reception following Theodore's swearing-in ceremony, Edith held a bouquet of flowers to avoid the exhausting task of shaking hands with 5,000 guests. This was a practice she followed for the rest of her husband's political ca-

Artist Tade Styka painted Theodore Roosevelt as a Rough Rider.

47

The Rough Riders

☆ ☆

The idea of fighting a war against Spanish rulers in Cuba appealed to Teddy Roosevelt's love of adventure. He also believed that America needed to flex its military muscles to become a world power. After President McKinley declared war on Spain in April 1898, Roosevelt rushed to resign his position as assistant secretary of the navy and prepare for battle. As was customary for officers of the time, he ordered his own uniform from an elegant New York shop. The jaunty image of the

mustachioed TR in his broad-brimmed hat, khaki fatigues, and polka-dot kerchief endures to this day. He then set about recruiting his own regiment, enlisting cowboys, Indians, frontiersmen, and college athletes who shared his macho enthusiasm. Known officially as the First United States Volunteer Cavalry, this gutsy group gained fame as the "Rough Riders." After several weeks of training in Florida, they shipped out to Cuba on June 14, 1898, itching to fight. Lieutenant Colonel Roosevelt led them in their famous charge up Kettle Hill into a barrage

of Spanish gunfire. With the help of troops from four black regiments, they took the ridges surrounding Santiago. The city surrendered two weeks later. While 89 Rough Riders were killed or wounded, the regiment's exploits captured America's imagination and made TR a popular hero.

Left to right: Ted (seated on floor with a family dog), Ethel, Alice (holding another dog), Quentin, Kermit (with a guinea pig), and Archie about 1899

reer. With the older children in school and the younger ones under Mame's care, Edith had more time for herself. She set about refurbishing the governor's official residence. She even had a gym built so that her husband could get the exercise he needed. She also joined a group of women who met to discuss the books they had read. With Theodore, she went to county fairs, concerts, and receptions, and entertained distinguished guests.

In early 1900, the Republican leaders were already discussing candidates

Theodore Roosevelt is shown at his desk when he was governor of New York.

for the upcoming presidential election. "I don't want to see him nominated for the vice presidency!" Edith told a dinner guest in Albany. For once, the Roosevelts were financially secure. They did not have to pay for the upkeep of their official residence, and Theodore was earning a decent salary. Unlike a New York governor, the vice president was not given a place to live, and his salary was lower. While Theodore was attracted to the idea of becoming vice president, he

A 1900 portrait of Governor Theodore Roosevelt

Big Sticks and Teddy Bears

★ ★

The rough-riding, big-game hunting Theodore Roosevelt left us a lot to remember him by. A popular hero since his adventures in the Spanish-American War, TR's reputation loomed large and colorful even in his own day. Everything about him was oversized: his broad smile, his energy, and his passion for life. "His personality so crowds the room that the walls threaten to burst," said a friend. He always had a clever remark to make. At home, he offered the people a "square deal." Abroad, he believed in "walking softly and carrying a big stick," to make the United States a world power. Because he loved the great outdoors and "the strenuous life," he ordered 148,000,000 acres (60,000,000 ha) of land and many natural wonders to be protected by the government. He established the United States Forest Service and five new national parks. In 1901, Roosevelt issued an executive order officially changing the name of the Executive Mansion to The White House. His is one of four presidential faces carved into Mount Rushmore. It was to commemorate Roosevelt's adoption of a bear cub that an enterprising toymaker created a small stuffed bear. When he asked permission to call his toy "Teddy Bear," the president responded: "I don't think my name is likely to be worth much in the bear business, but you are welcome to use it."

wanted to stay in Albany for another term to complete his reform program. Thinking the matter was settled, Edith took a trip to Cuba in the spring of 1900 to see the site of her husband's triumph. Her sister Emily went with her.

Edith had failed to take the Republican party leaders into account. They were disturbed by the governor's reform program because it was directed against big business, the backbone of the Republican party. They wanted to move Theodore to a less powerful po-

President William McKinley (left) and vice-presidential candidate Theodore Roosevelt discussing plans for the 1900 presidential campaign

sition, the vice presidency. In June, Edith helped her husband write a statement discouraging further talk of his leaving Albany for Washington.

Nevertheless, the crafty party leaders asked Theodore to second President William McKinley's renomination. As they anticipated, he was greeted with

Vice-presidential candidate Theodore Roosevelt speaking for the Republican ticket during a 1900 presidential campaign rally

hearty applause by his many admirers. After such a demonstration of support, Theodore could no longer resist demands that he become McKinley's running mate. In the election of 1900, he was elected vice president. Edith never dreamed that she would soon become a First Lady in a new century.

CHAPTER THREE

A First Lady in a New Century

"Today, for the first time I went to the White House . . . how unlikely it is that . . . I shall ever [again] come in contact with [it]," Edith had written to Conie in 1877. How wrong she was. President and Mrs. Grover Cleveland invited Edith and her husband to dinner at the Executive Mansion in 1895. Even after Theodore was sworn in as vice president in 1901, however, Edith had no reason to expect that the Roosevelt family would actually be living in the White House.

Six months later, Edith was on vacation with her children in the Adirondack Mountains when she

The Roosevelt family was vacationing in the Adirondacks (right) in September 1901 when they received word that President McKinley was not expected to survive an assassin's attack.

Alice Roosevelt clowning for the camera during the Roosevelts' 1901 vacation in the Adirondacks

56

received a frightening message from Theodore. He told her that on September 6, the president had been shot while visiting the Pan American Exposition in Buffalo. He added that he was abandoning his speaking tour to rush to McKinley's bedside. At first, the doctors believed McKinley would survive, so the vice president left Buffalo for the Adirondacks. Theodore was with his family when he learned that the president had taken a turn for the worse and was not expected to live. He returned to Buffalo.

On September 14, 1901, at the age of forty-two, Theodore became the youngest president to hold office in American history. Edith was not with him in Buffalo where he was sworn in. She and the children had already started out on the lengthy journey back to Sagamore Hill. She did accompany her husband to McKinley's funeral in Washington a few days later.

Edith found the family living quarters on the second floor of the White

President William McKinley was shot on September 6, 1901, during a visit to the Pan American Exposition.

Theodore's daughter Alice posing on the lawn of the White House

House unacceptably cramped and lacking in privacy. There wasn't enough space for her six children, ranging in age from three-and-a-half-year-old Quentin to seventeen-year-old Alice, as well as their numerous pets. To make matters worse, strangers constantly traipsed through the family's living quarters to meet with Theodore. Unfortunately, the president's office was next to the bedrooms. She decided to do something about these problems.

Archie (saluting) and Quentin (far right) with the White House Guard

President Roosevelt's office in the newly added West Wing of the White House

Early in 1902, Congress provided the funds for Edith to renovate the White House. At her direction, architects added a West Wing to the Executive Mansion for offices of the president and his staff. She also had them design a gallery where the portraits of First Ladies could be hung. The public rooms on the first floor were restored to the way they looked in Dolley Madison's time. Then Edith arranged to have cases built to display historic White House china. Finally,

President Roosevelt signing bills in his new White House office

she had a tennis court laid out so Theodore could get more exercise. While the reconstruction took place, the first family stayed at Sagamore Hill. Six months later, in November 1902, they moved back to the renovated White House.

Edith reorganized the staff so she could devote more time to her husband and children. To make the White House run efficiently, Edith put

At Edith's direction, the State Dining Room was enlarged so that it could seat more guests.

This lovely photograph of First Lady Edith Roosevelt was taken in 1901.

the chief usher in charge as a general manager. All the servants had to answer to him, and he reported to her. In addition, she used professional caterers to prepare meals for State dinner parties. After the State Dining Room was enlarged to seat more guests, the White House kitchen proved inadequate for formal banquets. Theodore, like all the presidents before him, had to pay all the bills for food, official entertaining, and domestic servants. The government eventually provided presidents with an allowance for these expenses.

In 1901, Edith hired Isabelle "Belle" Hagner to serve as her social secretary. This was an important first step in the development of the future office of the First Lady. Belle's salary was paid by the federal government. This gave additional importance to her duties. Among her responsibilities, Belle helped Edith decide whom to see and when. The First Lady completed control of her social schedule

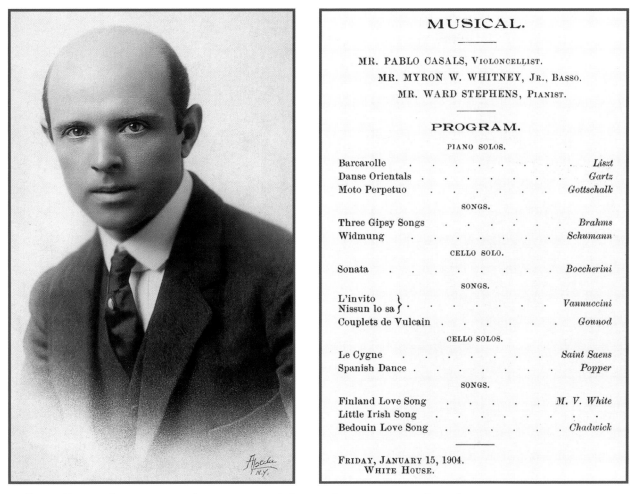

MUSICAL.

MR. PABLO CASALS, Violoncellist.
MR. MYRON W. WHITNEY, Jr., Basso.
MR. WARD STEPHENS, Pianist.

PROGRAM.

PIANO SOLOS.

Barcarolle	*Liszt*
Danse Orientals	*Gartz*
Moto Perpetuo	*Gottschalk*

SONGS.

Three Gipsy Songs	*Brahms*
Widmung	*Schumann*

CELLO SOLO.

Sonata	*Boccherini*

SONGS.

L'invito } Nissun lo sa }	*Vannuccini*
Couplets de Vulcain	*Gounod*

CELLO SOLOS.

Le Cygne	*Saint Saens*
Spanish Dance	*Popper*

SONGS.

Finland Love Song	*M. V. White*
Little Irish Song	
Bedouin Love Song	*Chadwick*

FRIDAY, JANUARY 15, 1904.
WHITE HOUSE.

Cellist Pablo Casals was among the musicians Edith invited to entertain at the White House.

by holding weekly meetings with the cabinet wives. (Members of the president's cabinet are the heads of government departments.) Under Edith's direction, the ladies coordinated their own party plans so that they would not conflict with White House events.

Invitations to the White House were in great demand. Edith's guest lists included artists and intellectuals as well as politicians and diplomats. Her musical evenings included great performers of the day, among them the brilliant young cellist Pablo Casals.

Booker T. Washington (1856–1915)

☆ ☆

Born a slave in Virginia, Booker Taliaferro (he added the Washington later) spent his first years of freedom after the Civil War toiling in a salt furnace and a coal mine. Determined to educate himself, he attended several schools and became a teacher. He believed in equality for black people and advocated patient self-improvement as the path to success. "It is at the bottom of life we must begin, and not at the top," he argued. Washington organized the Tuskegee Normal and Industrial Institute (now Tuskegee University) in Alabama in 1881 with thirty students and four run-down buildings. His goal was to teach black people the industrial and agricultural skills they would need to make good lives for themselves. By the time TR invited Washington to dinner at the White House in 1901, 1,400 students studied 30 different trades on a much larger Tuskegee campus. No wonder Roosevelt called Washington "the South's most distinguished citizen" and consulted him about appointing black people to federal jobs in the South. In those days, however, black Americans were not accepted by white society. When Washington's appearance at the presidential dinner table caused a major scandal, Roosevelt was genuinely surprised. The *New York Times* reported the exciting gossip surrounding the dinner party. As time went by, Washington's practical approach to equality struck many more-militant blacks as too limiting. His voice was soon drowned out by a new generation who believed in political activism and more aggressive tactics. Booker T. Washington, champion of hard work, died in 1915, exhausted by his own labors.

The Roosevelts restored formality to State receptions A fanfare of trumpets announced the arrival of the president and his wife. Edith held a bouquet so she would not have to shake hands with the numerous guests. No working people or black people were invited. Theodore, however, did ask Booker T. Washington, the head of Tuskegee Institute, to dine with him. Washington was the first African-American guest to visit the Executive Mansion.

In addition to her social duties, Belle helped with the First Lady's correspondence. Given her concern with privacy, Edith often asked those who received her personal letters to destroy them after they were read. She received many requests for government jobs or for financial help. She replied with a form letter, politely stating that she could not involve herself in politics. Nevertheless, she privately forwarded a few letters to government departments for action. Quietly and discreetly, she made many donations to the needy, often using others, such

President Theodore Roosevelt (standing) speaking at what was then called the Tuskegee Normal and Industrial Institute, founded by Booker T. Washington (seated, center right)

Artist Cecilia Beaux painted this portrait of Edith and her daughter Ethel.

as doctors in charity wards, to distribute money for her.

"One hates to feel that all one's life is public property," Edith wrote. Upper-class women of Edith's genera-tion believed their names should ap-pear in the newspapers only three times: to record their births, weddings, and deaths. She worked out a compro-mise between her wishes for privacy and the public's curiosity about her and her family. Edith relied on Belle to serve unofficially as the First Lady's press secretary. Edith chose a few pho-tographers to take pictures of herself and the children. Belle released them to the press upon request. The accom-panying stories focused on the presi-dent, not his family.

To Edith's dismay, Alice reveled in publicity and became a popular idol. The hit song of the era was "Alice Blue Gown," named for her and her favorite color. In 1902, the press la-beled her "Princess Alice" when she christened the German yacht of Prince Henry, brother of the German ruler, Kaiser Wilhelm. Her escapades were scandalous because they broke the social rules of the day. She smoked cigarettes in public, placed bets at racetracks, and drove a car from New-port to Boston without a chaperone. As a stepmother, Edith offered her af-fection but relied on Theodore to dis-

Mr. Gibson's Girls

✶ ✶

In the late 1880s, a beautiful young woman took the country by storm. She was tall and graceful with a lush head of hair arranged softly around her face. For twenty years, she reigned as the ideal of American womanhood. Women imitated her and men adored her. Who was she? She was the "Gibson Girl," an imaginary goddess drawn by illustrator Charles Dana Gibson. Soon after her image first appeared in *Life* magazine, the Gibson Girl set the standard for American beauty, fashion, and attitude. Her crisp white blouses and long dark skirts (which fell smoothly from her impossibly slender waist) were all the rage among stylish women. She played golf and tennis, drove a motorcar, and ignored the attentions of her handsome pen-and-ink suitors. Gibson originally created her to poke fun at the snobbery of the upper class, hardly imagining that her serialized exploits would have such broad appeal. Her face appeared on dishware, pillows, and even wallpaper. Finally, when the Roosevelts moved into the White House in 1901, Americans recognized a real Gibson Girl in the lovely and lively Alice. Indeed, TR's oldest daughter personified all of the looks, charm, and character of Mr. Gibson's imaginary beauty.

Alice Roosevelt was the image of the Gibson Girl

This Roosevelt family photograph was taken at Sagamore Hill in 1903. From left: Quentin, Theodore, Ted Jr., Archie, Alice, Kermit, Edith, and Ethel

cipline his headstrong daughter. "I can run the country or control Alice. I can't do both," was his reply to complaints about her conduct. As was the custom among members of the upper class, Alice was formally introduced to society when she reached marriageable age. Her debut was held at the White House in 1902. In 1908, her half-sister Ethel was given the less-lavish coming-out party she wanted.

In contrast to stories about Alice, stories about the younger children's antics were more wholesome. Kermit, the quietest of the group, had a kangaroo rat that demanded lumps of sugar at the breakfast table. When his brother Archie was sick, Quentin, the youngest child, smuggled their pony Algonquin into the White House elevator, down the second-floor corridor, and into Archie's bedroom to cheer him up. Quentin was the leader of the "White House Gang," a group of mischievous little boys. They decorated a portrait of Andrew Jackson with spitballs and scratched the newly polished ballroom floor by walking across it on stilts. Edith tolerated their pranks and rarely scolded them.

Archie on Algonquin, the pony Quentin smuggled into the ailing Archie's White House bedroom

Edith made a few concessions to modern technology. When Sagamore Hill became the Summer White House in 1901, a telephone was installed. On the other hand, the Roosevelts did not purchase a car until 1910 and did not replace gaslight with electricity until 1917. (The White House had telephones in 1877 and electric lights in 1889.) The president sometimes showed silent movies to his

69

Edith bought this cabin in Pine Knot, Virginia, in
1905 as a retreat for her and her husband.

guests at the Executive Mansion. On one occasion, Edith objected to the subject of a film: catching wild wolves barehanded. "How would you like to be asked to sit through a . . . performance of a lady showing antique fans?" she asked Theodore.

Despite their official duties and family responsibilities, Edith and Theodore managed to spend much time together. After breakfast with the children, they walked together in the garden. In the late af-

On Guard

* *

Edith Roosevelt often requested extra Secret Service agents to protect her husband, who avoided them whenever he could. Today, these vigilant guardians are specially trained to protect the president and the first family twenty-four hours a day anywhere in the world. The service actually began, however, as a kind of detective agency for the federal government. It was officially commissioned in 1865 to combat the counterfeiting of money that had become a major problem during the Civil War. The only national law-enforcement agency at that time, it soon took on other criminal investigations. Agents worked undercover to control extortion, forgery, lottery fraud, blackmail, and terrorism. After President William McKinley was assassinated (the third president to be murdered in office) in 1901, Congress added the job of protecting the chief executive. Over the years, the role expanded to include the First Lady, the presidential family, former presidents, and other dignitaries. While security is tight at the White House, the Secret Service faces its biggest challenges when the president travels. Every move must be mapped out and every inch of the way secured in advance. In crowds, agents surround the president to form a "safe zone." It is dangerous work; Secret Service agents know they must protect the president with their own lives if necessary.

ternoon, they often went riding. From her sitting room, Edith often called Theodore to come to bed when he worked past 10:30 at night.

In 1905, Edith bought a cabin called Pine Knot, in Virginia, 125 miles (201 km) from Washington, as a retreat for the president and herself. It was ideal for Theodore, who really enjoyed the rugged outdoor life. In those days, presidential couples did not have an official weekend getaway place. Now, the Roosevelts could enjoy brief periods of privacy. Nevertheless, Edith arranged for Secret Service protection without Theodore's knowledge. Ever since the McKinley assassination, she feared for his life.

Theodore consulted Edith on some of his political decisions but did not always take her advice. Edith was well informed. She read several newspapers each day, marking items for Theodore's attention. She also sorted his mail. To her dismay, however, he was more likely to ask for his sister Bamie's opinions. Theodore had always trusted Bamie's judgment.

In private, Edith did not hesitate to criticize Theodore when she thought he was making a mistake. She objected when Theodore appointed William Howard Taft as secretary of war in 1904. She felt he would not stand up to the president or give him impartial advice. Her judgment proved correct. When Theodore won election to the presidency in 1904, she disapproved of his announcement that he would not run again. She felt that Congress would use his statement as an excuse to ignore his requests for Progressive reforms. (Progressives used government power to bring about more democratic politics, fairer business competition, and safer working

Theodore Roosevelt taking the oath of office as president in 1905

A photograph of First Lady Edith Roosevelt in her inaugural gown

President Roosevelt (center) with the Russian and Japanese peace envoys, Ausust 19, 1905

conditions.) Despite Edith's misgivings, Congress did pass laws in 1906 that Theodore wanted them to pass. These ensured the safety and quality of the nation's food and drugs and regulated railroad rates.

Edith played an important role in helping her husband get information on the Russo-Japanese War of 1904–1905. A British diplomat in Russia, a longtime friend of the Roosevelts, wrote to Edith for over a year, supplying eyewitness accounts of conditions there for Theodore. It would have been inappropriate for him to write directly to the president. Then,

Noble Nobel

✮ ✮

Alfred Nobel was called the "Dynamite King." A Swedish inventor and chemist who lived in the 1800s, Nobel found a way to use the explosive nitroglycerin more safely by forming it into sticks. Strongly opposed to the military uses of his invention, called dynamite, he left money to fund the Nobel Prizes. Achievers in the areas of physics, chemistry, medicine, literature, economics, and peace receive what is now considered the highest honor in the world. The prizes were first awarded in 1901; in 1906, Theodore Roosevelt became the first American to receive one. As a promoter of peace, Alfred Nobel would be pleased to know that today more people associate him with the peace prize than with an explosive.

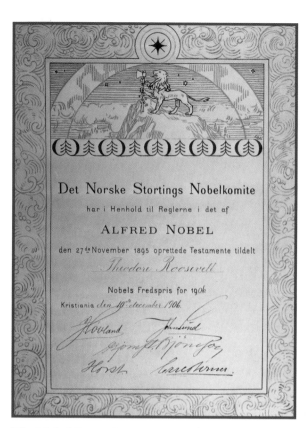

The Nobel Peace Prize was awarded to President Theodore Roosevelt in 1906.

Newlyweds Nicholas and Alice Roosevelt Longworth with Theodore (right)

Alice in her wedding gown the day of her elaborate White House wedding in 1906

when the timing was right, Theodore helped the Russians and Japanese negotiate a peace settlement. In 1906, he won the Nobel Prize for Peace for his efforts.

Because Theodore was president, even family weddings became public events. In 1905, Theodore gave his niece Eleanor in marriage to his fifth cousin Franklin D. Roosevelt. He

74

attracted more attention than the bride and groom. Eleanor had declined Edith's offer of a White House wedding and was married in New York. Alice, however, enjoyed the publicity she received when she married Ohio Congressman Nicholas Longworth in an elaborate White House wedding the following year. Edith was touched when her usually undemonstrative stepdaughter kissed her at the end of the ceremony.

Although she loved to travel, Edith had not campaigned with her husband during the election of 1904. Women were not expected to appear in public to ask for votes. In 1905, she did accompany Theodore on his speaking tour to strengthen support for the Republican party in the South and visited the plantation where his mother had grown up. She also went with him in 1906 to check on his most difficult project, the construction of the Panama Canal. In 1909, the Roosevelts greeted the Great White Fleet

Edith (second from right) accompanied Theodore (seated at left) to Panama in 1906 to check on the construction of the Panama Canal.

Digging the Big Ditch

✴ ✴

President Roosevelt left no larger legacy than the Panama Canal. In every way an example of the can-do spirit of America in the new twentieth century, the canal was an amazing engineering and political feat. Before its construction, ships traveling from New York to San Francisco sailed 13,000 miles (20,921 km) around the tip of South America. The canal made it possible to travel across the Isthmus of Panama, reducing the distance to 5,200 miles (8,368 km). Just a 50-mile (80-km) cut across a narrow neck of land was all it would take to connect the Atlantic and the Pacific Oceans. But the French had tried for nineteen years to dig the ditch, giving up when tropical diseases, inadequate tools, and political corruption got the better of them. In 1899, the United States embarked on several years of treaty making and negotiations to acquire the right to build and operate a canal. A revolution that won Panama independence from Colombia sealed the deal. Scientists worked hard at wiping out the malaria and yellow fever that made living and working in the region impossible. By the time construction was completed in 1914, more than 43,000 workers had dug 211 million cubic yards (161 million cubic meters) of earth through hills and swamps. TR's visit to the construction site in 1906 marked the first time an American president had set foot on foreign soil.

The Roosevelt family, including Alice and Nicholas Longworth (on the right), leaving the White House at the end of Theodore's term as president

in Hampton Roads, Virginia. The ships had just returned from a tour around the world in a show of U.S. naval power.

In 1909, as his term expired, Theodore was reluctant to leave office, but Edith said she was only "a little sad." She was looking forward to their years together in retirement. She wanted to give up Washington and become the first lady of Sagamore Hill.

This photograph of President Roosevelt and Edith was taken shortly before his term of office expired.

CHAPTER FOUR

First Lady of Sagamore Hill

✮ ✮ ✮ ✮ ✮ ✮ ✮ ✮ ✮ ✮ ✮ ✮ ✮ ✮ ✮ ✮

After leaving the White House, Edith commented, "I never realized what a strain I was under continuously until it was over." It wasn't really over for another year. First, Theodore left on an African safari and then the Roosevelts made a triumphal tour of Europe. Edith looked forward to enjoying the quiet life when they returned to Sagamore Hill in 1910. To her delight, Theodore decided to become an editor and an author to support his family. (Former presidents did not yet receive pensions when they left office.) At last, they would be private citizens, no longer pursued by the public, politicians, or reporters.

✮ ✮ ✮ ✮ ✮ ✮ ✮ ✮ ✮ ✮ ✮ ✮ ✮ ✮ ✮ ✮

Edith and Alice in Cambridge, England, in 1910

The quiet life, however, proved hazardous to Edith. In 1911, while galloping on horseback with her husband and son Archie, she was thrown from her horse. Unconscious for 36 hours, she wasn't completely aware of her surroundings for nine more days. As a result of the fall, she lost her sense of smell and never again enjoyed the aroma of flowers or the salt air of Oyster Bay. By then, Theodore had found the literary life too tame for him.

Edith never made public her opin-

This Roosevelt family portrait was taken in Oyster Bay in 1910.

William Howard Taft (1857–1930)

✮ ✮

Though friends, no two men could have been more different in style than President Theodore Roosevelt and his successor William Howard Taft. While Taft cut a large and imposing figure—he stood 6 feet (183 centimeters) and weighed over 300 pounds (136 kilograms)—his manner was gentle and pleasant. His first love was the law. A reluctant president, Taft knew that following the colorful Teddy into office would be a difficult assignment. William Howard Taft was born in Cincinnati, Ohio. He became a lawyer and married Helen Herron. Taft never wanted a political life and served happily in various judicial jobs until President McKinley made him governor of the Philippines in 1900. President Roosevelt later recruited him as his secretary of war. Elected president in 1908, Taft endured an unhappy four years, feeling underqualified and unable to fill TR's large shoes. His administration, however, was effective and efficient. To his relief, Taft did not win re-election in 1912 but went on to fulfill his heart's desire in 1921 when President Woodrow Wilson appointed him chief justice of the U.S. Supreme Court. William Howard Taft considered it the highest honor of his life.

ion of Theodore's decision to run for president in 1912. His friend and successor, President William Howard Taft, had failed to make more Progressive reforms. So Theodore challenged him for the Republican nomination, but lost. Edith loyally supported her husband when he formed the Progressive party, nicknamed the "Bull Moose" party after its leader, to seek the presidency. She approved of her husband's decision in 1912. She was-

This stunt photo of Theodore on a moose was taken during his 1912 presidential campaign as the nominee of the Bull Moose party.

Theodore giving a campaign speech in 1912

not happy about it, for personal reasons, but thought he was right in what he did, and that he had to do it for the good of the country. Years later, Edith wrote to one of her sons, "I have lived, most reluctantly, through one party split and no good comes of it."

In 1912, Theodore campaigned for women's suffrage. Edith had not favored the cause, but in 1912 for the first time she attended the Bull Moose convention and some political rallies. Earlier in her husband's career, women were not expected to take part in political campaigns, and some still felt that way in 1912. Edith did not join Theodore on his speaking tours around the nation to win votes. On October 14, 1912, she was at a New York theater when a young cousin whispered to her that Theodore had been shot, her worst fear as First Lady. She was relieved to be told that her husband had gone on to give his speech in Milwaukee. Since she assumed he was not seriously hurt, she stayed for the rest of the play. Later that evening, she learned that he had given his speech with a bullet lodged in his chest. Then he was taken to a hospital in Chicago.

Arriving at his bedside on October 16, she immediately took charge. To Theodore's dismay, she cleared his room of well-meaning but exhausting visitors. She insisted that he obey his doctors' orders. "This thing about ours being a campaign against boss rule is a fake," he told a reporter while smiling at his wife. "I never was so boss-ruled in my life as I am at this moment." (Bosses were corrupt politicians who traded political favors for money and votes to keep their own political organizations in power.) Theodore recovered, but Democrat Woodrow Wilson won the election.

At Sagamore Hill, the Roosevelts celebrated the weddings of their children and later rejoiced in visits from their fifteen grandchildren. Like many grandparents, however, Edith commented, "I like to see their little faces, but I prefer to see their backs." Having young ones around could prove very

Theodore, Archie, Edith, and Quentin at Sagamore Hill in 1914

A 1918 picture of Theodore (holding grandson Archie Roosevelt Jr.), Archie's mother Grace, Edith (behind grandson Richard Derby Jr.), and Ethel Roosevelt Derby (holding daughter Edith)

Edith and Theodore with their grandson, Richard Derby Jr.

exhausting for her, but Theodore still romped with them. Edith was uneasy when her husband left on a trip with son Kermit to explore an uncharted river in Brazil in 1913. The adventure nearly cost Theodore his life and left him subject to recurring fevers and illnesses. Edith was relieved when he returned to Sagamore Hill to recuperate and take up his literary career.

During the summer of 1914, like most Americans, Edith paid little attention to the outbreak of World War I between the Allies (Great Britain, France, and Russia) and the Central Powers (Germany and Austria-Hungary). In 1915–1916, German submarines preyed on U.S. shipping. This prompted Theodore to write a book urging the nation to prepare for war. Edith gave him the title, *Fear God and Take Your Own Part*. The United

World War I: Fast Facts

WHAT: The "Great War," the "War to End All Wars," the first truly global conflict

WHEN: 1914–1918

WHO: The Central European Powers, including Austria-Hungary and Germany, opposed the Allied Powers, including Britain, France, and Russia. The United States entered the war on the Allied side in 1917.

WHERE: The Central Powers invaded Serbia, Romania, Russia, Belgium, France, and Italy. Fighting extended into the Atlantic Ocean and the Mediterranean Sea.

WHY: European disputes over land, economics, religion and leadership boiled over in 1914 when Austrian archduke Francis Ferdinand was assassinated on a visit to Serbia. Austria declared war on Serbia, and other European nations joined in. The United States got involved largely because German submarine warfare disrupted commerce in the North Atlantic Ocean.

OUTCOME: The Central Powers fell to the Allied Powers in 1918, and an armistice was signed on November 11. The map of Europe was redrawn and the League of Nations was founded to settle international disputes. Ten million soldiers, including 116,500 Americans, had died.

World War I photos of the German kaiser with his sons (top) and Theodore with his sons

Theodore Roosevelt addressing soldiers before they went off to France during World War I

States entered the conflict on the Allied side in April 1917.

The Roosevelts soon became the proud parents of four servicemen. Archie, Ted Jr., and Kermit were decorated for their bravery under fire. Pride soon turned to sorrow, however. In July 1918, news arrived that Quentin had been killed when his plane was shot down by German

fighter pilots. Despite her grief, Edith realized, "You cannot bring up boys as eagles and expect them to turn out sparrows." She found some comfort in time spent with Theodore.

Four months later, Edith's self-discipline and strength of character were tested again. Saddened by the loss of his son, Theodore lost his enthusiasm for life. He entered Roosevelt Hospital

Theodore's flag-draped coffin in the East Room of the White House

in New York City on November 11, 1918. That was the day the armistice was signed, bringing an end to World War I. With Edith in attendance for the next 44 days, Theodore was treated for rheumatism, a sometimes crippling disease of the joints. When he came home, he was very weak and in constant pain. "I wonder if you will ever know how much I love Sagamore Hill," he said to Edith. Early the next morning, on January 6, 1919, he died in his sleep.

Edith lived for another twenty-nine years without Theodore. During her marriage to him, she was more interested in her family than in politics. In 1920, however, she got involved in politics to support his party and defend the Roosevelt family name. She took up her pen to urge women to cast their ballots for Republican presidential candidate Warren Harding. Although Edith had not been a supporter of women's rights, she realized that American women were coming into their own. As a result of the Nineteenth Amendment, this was the

Votes for Women!

☆ ☆ ☆ ☆ ☆ ☆ ☆ ☆ ☆ ☆ ☆ ☆ ☆ ☆ ☆ ☆ ☆ ☆ ☆ ☆

The women of America scored a great victory with the passage of the Nineteenth Amendment to the Constitution in 1920. Finally, they would be allowed to vote! Although many states had already given some voting rights to women, this watershed amendment guaranteed that: "The right of the citizens of the United States to vote shall not be denied or abridged by the the United States or any State on account of sex."

The battle for the right to vote had been long and bitter. Its organized roots can be traced to the first convention for women's rights held in Seneca Falls, New York, in 1848. Inspired by the growing movement to abolish slavery, convention delegates believed in equal rights for women under the law. Using the powerful language of the Declaration of Independence, they drafted a manifesto of women's rights called the Declaration of Sentiments.

For the next 72 years, many women, including Susan B. Anthony and Elizabeth Cady Stanton, worked tirelessly to achieve equal rights, including the vote, for women.

Over the years, the movement faced major opposition. Some people believed that women weren't smart enough to vote. Others feared that allowing women to vote would destroy the fabric of family life.

A woman suffrage, or right to vote, amendment was first introduced in Congress in 1878. Unbelievably, when it failed to pass, it was reintroduced in *every session* over the next 40 years, falling short each time. The movement itself was split by disagreements. Finally, in 1900, feminists united under the banner of the National American Woman Suffrage Association. As a result, the movement developed a spirit of unity and plunged ahead toward suffrage. During World War I, women's efforts on the homefront showed how capable they were. In 1920, the 2 million members of the Woman Suffrage Association, and all American women, reaped the fruits of years of hard work to win the vote.

A sampler made by Edith in 1925

Edith with her son Kermit in Japan, 1924

first time women nationwide could vote in a presidential election. Because the public mistakenly believed that Democratic vice presidential candidate Franklin D. Roosevelt was her son, loyal Republicans Edith and Ted Jr. frequently spoke out against him. Political feuds between the two Roosevelt families continued into the next decade.

Reading, sewing clothes for the poor at the Oyster Bay Needlework Guild, and participating in the local Republican club failed to fill Edith's days. To amuse herself, Edith became a world traveler, accompanied by members of her family. In 1919, on her first visit to Europe as a widow, she made arrangements for a memorial to Quentin in France. Other travels took her to South America and South Africa. Among her more interesting trips was a 1924 visit to Osaka, Japan, a few months after a devastating earthquake. She bravely endured the aftershocks before leaving for China. Then she boarded the Trans-Siberian Railroad for a 6,000-mile (9,656-km) trip across Russia to Moscow. Since Theodore left office, both Russia and

China had overthrown their imperial rulers and become republics. Finding the new regimes grim, Edith toured the former rulers' palaces. She shared her experiences in a book she wrote with Kermit, *Cleared for Strange Ports*, published in 1927.

During the remainder of her life, Edith willingly helped authors with their books about her husband, but in 1923, she destroyed most of Theodore's letters to her. Having strangers read them struck her as a terrible invasion of her privacy. Yet she was willing to share her own family's history with the public. On a car trip through Connecticut in 1920, she had stopped at the small town of Brooklyn, the home of her Tyler ancestors. Stimulated by her visit, she began writing a book with Kermit, tracing the history of the Tylers and the Carows in North America. *American Backlogs* was published in 1928. The year before, Edith had purchased Mortlake Manor, an inn built for her Tyler great grandfather. She stayed there every summer.

Edith could easily afford a second home. In addition to the money she had inherited, she received benefits as a presidential widow. In 1919, to honor Theodore's memory, Congress granted her the franking privilege, allowing her letters to be mailed and delivered without postage stamps. She also accepted a yearly pension set up by industrialist Andrew Carnegie in 1919 for presidential widows. She did not need the money, but she took it lest Carnegie withdraw his offer. She wanted the funds to be available to widowed First Ladies less fortunate than she. In 1928, Congress voted into law a measure similar to Carnegie's. Again, for the sake of other presidential widows, Edith convinced herself to accept it. She gave the money away to needy former "Rough Riders," struggling poets, and utter strangers.

In 1929, the stock market crashed, bringing the American economy to a halt in the Great Depression. Businesses closed and nearly 13 million workers lost their jobs. Unlike most Americans, Edith's investments were still sound so she did not have to worry about money. In 1932, as a dedicated Republican, she campaigned for President Herbert Hoover's reelec-

Edith at Madison Square Garden in 1932 making a campaign speech for President Hoover's reelection

lowing in his father's footsteps, Ted, a former assistant secretary of the navy, had run for governor of New York in 1924. Franklin's wife Eleanor, a New York Democratic party leader, set out to help Democrat Alfred E. Smith defeat him and succeeded. Ted later became governor-general of the Philippines, but in 1933, the victorious President Franklin Roosevelt removed him from office.

Ted Jr. campaigning in 1924 for the governorship of New York, a campaign he lost

tion. He was in office when the Great Depression began. The newsreel cameras filmed her departing by plane for a White House luncheon. Millions of Americans in movie theaters later heard her say, "I'm on my way to Washington." She also gave a speech at Madison Square Garden urging voters to support Hoover. His opponent was Franklin D. Roosevelt.

In part, Edith supported Hoover in order to avenge her son Ted Jr. Fol-

Edith never approved of Franklin's "New Deal," government programs to give relief to the needy, to reform businesses, and to employ workers. Like many Republicans in the 1930s, she felt that these measures were "incompatible with American democracy and liberty." In September 1935, on the 146th anniversary of the adoption of the U.S. Constitution, she made a radio broadcast asking people to return to the ideals of George Washington. As a loyal Republican, she supported Franklin's Republican opponent Alfred Landon in the election of 1936. He lost.

In December 1941, after the Japanese surprise air raid on Pearl Harbor Hawaii, the United States entered World War II (1939–1945). Edith's three remaining sons rejoined the U.S. forces. They fought beside the Allies (Britain, France, China, and the Soviet Union) against the Axis (Germany, Italy, and Japan) all over the globe. Archie alone survived. He earned a Silver Star for his heroism in New Guinea, an island in the Western Pacific Ocean. Kermit, an alcoholic stationed in Alaska, committed sui-

Edith made a radio broadcast in 1935 on the anniversary of the adoption of the U.S. Constitution.

cide in June 1943. Edith was told he died of heart failure. Ted received the Congressional Medal of Honor for his leadership on D-Day, June 6, 1944, when the Allies landed on the French Coast. He died of a heart attack a month later. Edith was devastated by the loss of her two sons. Yet she found the strength to write a note of comfort to Eleanor when President Roosevelt died on April 12, 1945. During the war, she had mellowed toward Cousin Franklin, admitting that he was "a nice man," even though he was "on the wrong side" politically.

World War II: Fast Facts

WHAT: The second great global conflict

WHEN: 1939–1945

WHO: The Axis Powers, including Germany, Italy, and Japan, opposed the Allies, including Britain, France, and the USSR. The United States entered the war on the Allied side in 1941 after Japan bombed the American naval base at Pearl Harbor in Hawaii.

WHERE: Fighting raged throughout the Pacific Ocean and in the Atlantic, as well as from Scandinavia to North Africa, and deep into the Soviet Union.

WHY: Chancellor Adolf Hitler set out to make Germany the most powerful country in the world, and began by invading his European neighbors. Japan, Italy, and Germany pledged support to one another in 1940. When the United States declared war on Japan after the attack on Pearl Harbor in 1941, Germany and Italy declared war on the United States.

OUTCOME: The war ended in stages. Germany surrendered in May 1945. Japan surrendered after the United States dropped two atomic bombs there in August. More than 400,000 American troops died in battle; about 17 million on both sides perished.

Edith's sons during World War II, from left to right: Lieutenant Colonel Archie Roosevelt, Major Kermit Roosevelt, Brigadier General Theodore Roosevelt Jr.

By war's end, in the fall of 1945, Edith was quite fragile. She survived three more years, weak and bedridden with hardening of the arteries and shortness of breath. She died in the early morning of September 30, 1948, at the age of eighty-seven. Only her name and the dates of her birth and death are inscribed on her tombstone. She had wanted it to read: "Everything she did was for the happiness of others." This would have been a more fitting tribute to a caring wife and mother who was also a very capable First Lady.

Edith in 1943, five years before her death

Portrait of America, 1948: Frozen Food and Cold War

✫ ✫

Edith Carow Roosevelt's life had taken her from the Civil War to the Cold War. When she died, the world was still recovering from World War II. Confusion in war-torn Europe led to a power struggle there between Western nations and Russia, also known by then as the Soviet Union. When the powerful Soviet Union drew an "Iron Curtain" around a large bloc of countries that had fallen to communism, an icy chill fell over the world. The Cold War had begun.

In June 1948, events came close to war when the Soviet Union blockaded the city of Berlin, Germany, by cutting off all rail and road traffic there. They hoped the Americans, British, and French would abandon the city and leave it in Soviet hands. Instead, those nations launched a fleet of cargo planes and dropped tons of food and supplies every day to the city. Several months later, the Soviets ended the blockade.

The successful airlift helped President Harry Truman win a surprising re-election that year. Around the 48 states, Americans were working toward the good life that the booming post-war economy promised. Young couples flocked to brand-new suburban residential communities where rows and rows of identical houses could be bought for about $6,990 each. In these little houses, young families lived the American dream and started the baby boom. In California, the McDonald Brothers opened a revolutionary drive-through where hamburgers cost fifteen cents each. In sports, the National Basketball Association was born, and super-slugger George Herman "Babe" Ruth died of cancer at age fifty-three.

Even in this age before rock 'n' roll, Americans loved their music, enjoying hits by crooners and jazz musicians. Americans couldn't get enough television, either. Still in its infancy, TV offered variety and talent shows, boxing and roller derbies to an audience eager to be entertained.

In spite of the peace and prosperity, however, Americans feared the growing threat of communism. This fear would shape people's lives for years to come.

The Presidents and Their First Ladies

President	Birth–Death	First Lady	Birth–Death
YEARS IN OFFICE			
1789–1797			
George Washington	1732–1799	Martha Dandridge Custis Washington	1731–1802
1797–1801			
John Adams	1735–1826	Abigail Smith Adams	1744–1818
1801–1809			
Thomas Jefferson†	1743–1826		
1809–1817			
James Madison	1751–1836	Dolley Payne Todd Madison	1768–1849
1817–1825			
James Monroe	1758–1831	Elizabeth Kortright Monroe	1768–1830
1825–1829			
John Quincy Adams	1767–1848	Louisa Catherine Johnson Adams	1775–1852
1829–1837			
Andrew Jackson†	1767–1845		
1837–1841			
Martin Van Buren†	1782–1862		
1841			
William Henry Harrison‡	1773–1841		
1841–1845			
John Tyler	1790–1862	Letitia Christian Tyler (1841–1842)	1790–1842
		Julia Gardiner Tyler (1844–1845)	1820–1889
1845–1849			
James K. Polk	1795–1849	Sarah Childress Polk	1803–1891
1849–1850			
Zachary Taylor	1784–1850	Margaret Mackall Smith Taylor	1788–1852
1850–1853			
Millard Fillmore	1800–1874	Abigail Powers Fillmore	1798–1853
1853–1857			
Franklin Pierce	1804–1869	Jane Means Appleton Pierce	1806–1863
1857–1861			
James Buchanan*	1791–1868		
1861–1865			
Abraham Lincoln	1809–1865	Mary Todd Lincoln	1818–1882
1865–1869			
Andrew Johnson	1808–1875	Eliza McCardle Johnson	1810–1876
1869–1877			
Ulysses S. Grant	1822–1885	Julia Dent Grant	1826–1902
1877–1881			
Rutherford B. Hayes	1822–1893	Lucy Ware Webb Hayes	1831–1889
1881			
James A. Garfield	1831–1881	Lucretia Rudolph Garfield	1832–1918
1881–1885			
Chester A. Arthur†	1829–1886		

† wife died before he took office   ‡ wife too ill to accompany him to Washington   * never married

1885–1889			
Grover Cleveland	1837–1908	Frances Folsom Cleveland	1864–1947
1889–1893			
Benjamin Harrison	1833–1901	Caroline Lavinia Scott Harrison	1832–1892
1893–1897			
Grover Cleveland	1837–1908	Frances Folsom Cleveland	1864–1947
1897–1901			
William McKinley	1843–1901	Ida Saxton McKinley	1847–1907
1901–1909			
Theodore Roosevelt	1858–1919	Edith Kermit Carow Roosevelt	1861–1948
1909–1913			
William Howard Taft	1857–1930	Helen Herron Taft	1861–1943
1913–1921			
Woodrow Wilson	1856–1924	Ellen Louise Axson Wilson (1913–1914)	1860–1914
		Edith Bolling Galt Wilson (1915–1921)	1872–1961
1921–1923			
Warren G. Harding	1865–1923	Florence Kling Harding	1860–1924
1923–1929			
Calvin Coolidge	1872–1933	Grace Anna Goodhue Coolidge	1879–1957
1929–1933			
Herbert Hoover	1874–1964	Lou Henry Hoover	1874–1944
1933–1945			
Franklin D. Roosevelt	1882–1945	Anna Eleanor Roosevelt	1884–1962
1945–1953			
Harry S. Truman	1884–1972	Bess Wallace Truman	1885–1982
1953–1961			
Dwight D. Eisenhower	1890–1969	Mamie Geneva Doud Eisenhower	1896–1979
1961–1963			
John F. Kennedy	1917–1963	Jacqueline Bouvier Kennedy	1929–1994
1963–1969			
Lyndon B. Johnson	1908–1973	Claudia Taylor (Lady Bird) Johnson	1912–
1969–1974			
Richard Nixon	1913–1994	Patricia Ryan Nixon	1912–1993
1974–1977			
Gerald Ford	1913–	Elizabeth Bloomer Ford	1918–
1977–1981			
James Carter	1924–	Rosalynn Smith Carter	1927–
1981–1989			
Ronald Reagan	1911–	Nancy Davis Reagan	1923–
1989–1993			
George Bush	1924–	Barbara Pierce Bush	1925–
1993–			
William Jefferson Clinton	1946–	Hillary Rodham Clinton	1947–

Edith Kermit Carow Roosevelt
Timeline

1861	★	Civil War begins
		Edith Kermit Carow is born on August 6
1863	★	Emancipation Proclamation goes into effect
		President Abraham Lincoln gives the Gettysburg Address
1864	★	Abraham Lincoln is reelected president
1865	★	Edith Kermit Carow meets Theodore Roosevelt
		The Civil War ends
		Abraham Lincoln is assassinated
		Andrew Johnson becomes president
1866	★	Final transatlantic cable is laid between Great Britain and the United States
1867	★	United States purchases Alaskan territory from Russia
1868	★	Ulysses S. Grant is elected president
		Louisa May Alcott's *Little Women* is published
		Edith Kermit Carow attends kindergarten at the Roosevelt's home
1869	★	National Women Suffrage Association is formed
1871	★	Fire destroys most of Chicago
1872	★	Susan B. Anthony is arrested for trying to vote
		Ulysses S. Grant is reelected president
		Yellowstone National Park becomes the first U.S. national park
1873	★	Economic depression spreads throughout the United States
1876	★	George Armstrong Custer and his troops are killed at the Battle of the Little Big Horn
1877	★	Rutherford B. Hayes becomes president

1879	★	Women win the right to argue cases before the Supreme Court
1880	★	Theodore Roosevelt marries Alice Hathaway Lee James Garfield is elected president
1881	★	James A. Garfield is shot and dies about three months later Chester A. Arthur becomes president
1882	★	Congress approves a pension for widows of U.S. presidents
1884	★	Theodore Roosevelt's daughter Alice is born Theodore Roosevelt's wife Alice dies Grover Cleveland is elected president
1885	★	Washington Monument is dedicated Edith Carow and Theodore Roosevelt renew their friendship

1886	★	Statue of Liberty is dedicated Edith Kermit Carow marries Theodore Roosevelt
1887	★	Theodore Roosevelt Jr. is born
1888	★	Benjamin Harrison is elected president
1889	★	Kermit Roosevelt is born
1891	★	Populist party is formed Ethel Roosevelt is born
1892	★	Ellis Island immigration center opens Grover Cleveland is elected president
1893	★	Economic depression hits the United States
1894	★	Archibald Roosevelt is born
1895	★	Cuba begins a revolt against Spain

1896	★	William McKinley is elected president
1897	★	Quentin Roosevelt is born
1898	★	Spanish-American War is fought, resulting in the United States annexing Puerto Rico, Guam, and the Philippines

99

1900	✯	William McKinley is reelected president
		Theodore Roosevelt is elected vice president
1901	✯	President McKinley is assassinated
		Theodore Roosevelt becomes president
1902	✯	Cuba wins independence from Spain
1903	✯	Panama and the United States sign a treaty for the building of the Panama Canal
1904	✯	Theodore Roosevelt is elected president
1905	✯	Russo-Japanese War is fought and President Roosevelt helps negotiate peace
1906	✯	Theodore Roosevelt receives the Nobel Peace Prize
1908	✯	William Howard Taft is elected president
1909	✯	National Association for the Advancement of Colored People (NAACP) is founded
1912	✯	Theodore Roosevelt forms the Progressive party and runs for president
		Woodrow Wilson is elected president
1913	✯	Henry Ford sets up his first assembly line
1914	✯	Panama Canal is completed
		World War I begins
1916	✯	Woodrow Wilson is reelected president
		National Park Service is established
1917	✯	United States enters World War I
1918	✯	United States and its allies win World War I
1919	✯	Theodore Roosevelt dies on January 6
1920	✯	Nineteenth Amendment, which gave women the right to vote, is added to the U.S. Constitution
		Warren G. Harding is elected president
		Woodrow Wilson receives the Nobel Peace Prize for working out the peace after World War I
1923	✯	President Harding dies
		Calvin Coolidge becomes president

1924	★	Calvin Coolidge is elected president
1927	★	Charles Lindbergh flies solo across the Atlantic Ocean
1928	★	Herbert Hoover is elected president
		Amelia Earhart becomes the first woman to fly across the Atlantic Ocean
1929	★	Stock market crashes, which starts the Great Depression
1931	★	"The Star-Spangled Banner" becomes the national anthem
1932	★	Amelia Earhart becomes the first woman to fly solo across the Atlantic Ocean
		Franklin D. Roosevelt is elected president
1933	★	President Roosevelt begins the New Deal
1935	★	Congress passes the Social Security Act
1936	★	Franklin D. Roosevelt is reelected president
1939	★	World War II begins
1940	★	Franklin D. Roosevelt is reelected president
1941	★	Japanese bomb Pearl Harbor
		United States enters World War II
1944	★	Franklin D. Roosevelt is reelected president
1945	★	President Roosevelt dies
		Harry S. Truman becomes president
		Germany surrenders to the Allies in Europe
		United States drops atomic bombs on Japan
		Japan surrenders, ending World War II
1947	★	Jackie Robinson becomes the first African American to play major league baseball
1948	★	Harry S. Truman is elected president
		Edith Kermit Carow Roosevelt dies on September 30

Fast Facts about
Edith Kermit Carow Roosevelt

Born: August 6, 1861, in Norwich, Connecticut

Died: September 30, 1948, at Oyster Bay, New York

Burial Site: Oyster Bay, New York

Parents: Charles Carow and Gertrude Tyler Carow

Education: Private kindergarten at the Roosevelts' home; Miss Comstock's School

Marriage: To Theodore Roosevelt on December 2, 1886, until his death on January 6, 1919

Children: Theodore Jr., Kermit, Ethel, Archibald, and Quentin

Stepdaughter: Alice Roosevelt

Places She Lived: Norwich, Connecticut (1861–1864); New York City (1864–1889, 1895–1897); Sagamore Hill in Oyster Bay, New York (1887–1948); Washington, D.C. (1889–1895, 1897–1899, 1901–1910); Albany, New York (1899–1901); Pine Knot, Virginia (1905–1910); summers in Red Bank, New Jersey (1874–1877), Oyster Bay, New York (1874–1877), Mortlake Manor in Brooklyn, Connecticut (1927–1948)

Major Achievements:
* Renovated the White House by adding the West Wing for the president and his staff, the gallery for portraits of First Ladies, and a tennis court; enlarged the State Dining Room to seat more guests.
* Reorganized the duties of the White House staff and restored a formal atmosphere to State receptions.
* Began the tradition of a staff for the First Lady by hiring a social secretary who also acted as a press secretary and who was paid by the federal government.
* Helped her husband gain information about the Russo-Japanese War (1905) for which he negotiated the peace and later won the Nobel Peace Prize (1906).
* Prepared the White House wedding for her stepdaughter, Alice.
* Campaigned in presidential elections for Warren Harding and Herbert Hoover.
* With her son Kermit, wrote two books: *Cleared for Strange Ports* (1927) and *American Backlogs* (1928).

Fast Facts about
Theodore Roosevelt's Presidency

Terms of Office: Became the twenty-sixth president of the United States upon the death of President William McKinley on September 14, 1901; elected president in his own right in 1904 and served until March 4, 1909

Vice President: No vice president from September 14, 1901, to March 4, 1905; Charles Warren Fairbanks (1905–1909)

Major Policy Decisions and Legislation:
* Became known as the trust buster, after he broke up a large railroad trust (1902).
* Helped end a coal strike (1902) by forcing the mine owners to back down, and then appointed a commission that gave the miners a pay raise.
* Issued proclamations that set aside forests in Idaho, Wyoming, Arizona, Montana, and Alaska as national preserves (1902).
* Acquired land from the government of Panama (1903) for building the Panama Canal, and closely monitored the building of the canal.
* Urged Russia and Japan to stop the Russo-Japanese War and suggested a peace conference, which was held in August 1905.
* Supported and signed many reform laws, including the Pure Food and Drug Act and the Meat Inspection Act (both in 1906).

Major Events:
* President Theodore Roosevelt appointed three associate justices, who were confirmed, to the U.S. Supreme Court: Oliver Wendell Holmes (December 4, 1902); William Rufus Day (February 23, 1903); William Henry Moody (December 12, 1906).
* Became the first president to be submerged in a submarine (August 25, 1905, off Oyster Bay, New York).
* Was awarded the Nobel Peace Prize in December 1906 for his role in ending the Russo-Japanese War.
* Sent the U.S. fleet on an around-the-world cruise (1907–1909) to show U.S. naval power to other countries.

Where to Visit

The Capitol Building
Constitution Avenue
Washington, D.C. 20510
(202) 225-3121

Museum of American History of the
    Smithsonian Institution
"First Ladies: Political and Public Image"
14th Street and Constitution Ave. NW
Washington, D.C.
(202) 357-2008

National Archives
Constitution Avenue
Washington, D.C. 20408
(202) 501-5000

The National First Ladies Library
The Saxton McKinley House
331 South Market Avenue
Canton, Ohio 44702

Sagamore Hill National Historic Site
20 Sagamore Hill Road
Oyster Bay, New York 11771

Theodore Roosevelt Birthplace National
    Historic Site
28 East 20th Street
New York, New York 10003

White House
1600 Pennsylvania Avenue
Washington, D.C. 20500
Visitor's Office: (202) 456-7041

White House Historical Association
740 Jackson Place NW
Washington, D.C. 20503
(202) 737-8292

Online Sites of Interest

The First Ladies of the United States of America
http://www2.whitehouse.gov/WH/glimpse/ firstladies/html/firstladies.html
A portrait and biographical sketch of each First Lady plus links to other White House sites

Internet Public Library, Presidents of the United States (IPL POTUS)
http://www.ipl.org/ref/POTUS/troosevelt. html
A site with much information on Theodore Roosevelt, including personal information and facts about his presidency; many links to other sites including biographies and other Internet resources

The National First Ladies Library
http://www.firstladies.org
The first virtual library devoted to the lives and legacies of America's First Ladies; includes a bibliography of material by and about the nation's First Ladies, a tour of the Saxton McKinley House in Canton, Ohio, which houses the library

Sagamore Hill National Historic Site
http://www.town-of-oyster-bay.org/ interest/sagamore.htm
A description and photo of the last per-manent home of Theodore Roosevelt, in Oyster Bay, New York

Theodore Roosevelt National Park
http://www.nps.gov/thro/tr_visit.htm
Located in the Badlands of North Dakota, this was the place Roosevelt dis-covered as a young man and where he loved to live the life of a cowboy, explore, and renew his spirit.

The White House
http://www.whitehouse.gov/WH/Welcome. html
Information about the current president and vice president; White House history and tours; biographies of past presidents and their families; a virtual tour of the historic building, current events, and much more

The White House for Kids
http://www.whitehouse.gov/WH/kids/html/ kidshome.html
Socks the cat is your guide to this site, which includes information about White House kids, past and present; famous "First Pets," past and present; historic moments of the presidency; several issues of a newsletter called "Inside the White House," and more.

For Further Reading

Carter, Alden R. *The Spanish-American War*. New York: Franklin Watts, 1992.

Fritz, Jean. *Bully for You, Teddy Roosevelt!* New York: G.P. Putnam's Sons, 1991.

Gormley, Beatrice. *First Ladies*. New York: Scholastic, Inc., 1997.

Gould, Lewis L. (ed.). *American First Ladies: Their Lives and Their Legacy*. New York: Garland Publishing, 1996.

Guzzetti, Paula. *The White House*. Parsippany, N.J.: Silver Burdett Press, 1995.

Jacobson, Doranne. *Presidents and First Ladies of the United States*. New York: Smithmark Publishers, Inc., 1995.

Kay, Helen. *The First Teddy Bear*. Owings Mill, Maryland: Stemmer House Publishers, Inc., 1985.

Kent, Zachary. *The Rough Riders*. Cornerstones of Freedom series. Chicago: Children's Press, 1991.

———. *Theodore Roosevelt: Twenty-Sixth President of the United States*. Encyclopedia of Presidents series. Chicago: Children's Press, 1988.

Klapthor, Margaret Brown. *The First Ladies*. 8th edition. Washington, D.C.: White House Historical Association, 1995.

Mann, Elizabeth. *The Panama Canal: The Story of How a Jungle Was Conquered and the World Made Smaller*. Wonders of the World series. New York: Mikaya Press, 1998.

Mayo, Edith P. (ed.). *The Smithsonian Book of the First Ladies: Their Lives, Times, and Issues*. New York: Henry Holt, 1996.

Sandak, Cass R. *The Theodore Roosevelts*. First Families series. New York: Crestwood House, 1991.

Index

Page numbers in **boldface type** indicate illustrations

Photo Identifications

Cover: Portrait of Edith Roosevelt as First Lady
Page 8: Portrait of Edith Kermit Carow in 1868
Page 26: Portrait of Edith Carow in 1885
Page 54: Portrait of Edith Roosevelt as First Lady; portrait of President Theodore Roosevelt by John Singer Sargent
Page 78: Portrait of Edith Roosevelt by De Laszlo

Photo Credits©

About the Author

Barbara Silberdick Feinberg graduated with honors from Wellesley College where she was elected to Phi Beta Kappa. She holds a Ph.D. in political science from Yale University. Among her more recent books are *Watergate: Scandal in the White House; American Political Scandals Past and Present; The National Government; State Governments; Local Governments; Words in the News: A Student's Dictionary of American Government and Politics; Harry S. Truman; John Marshall: The Great Chief Justice; Electing the President; The Cabinet; Hiroshima and Nagasaki; Black Tuesday: The Stock Market Crash of 1929; Term Limits for Congress; The Constitutional Amendments; Next in Line: The American Vice Presidency;* and two previous books in the Encyclopedia of First Ladies series: *Patricia Ryan Nixon* and *Bess Wallace Truman.* She has also written *Marx and Marxism; The Constitution: Yesterday, Today, and Tomorrow;* and *Franklin D. Roosevelt, Gallant President.* She is a contributor to *The Young Reader's Companion to American History.*

Mrs. Feinberg lives in New York City with her younger son Douglas and two Yorkshire terriers, Katie and Holly. Among her hobbies are growing African violets, collecting antique autographs of historical personalities, listening to the popular music of the 1920s and 1930s, and working out in exercise classes.